TEACHER

by Sheila Rivera

first step nonfiction

Lerner Publications · Minneapolis

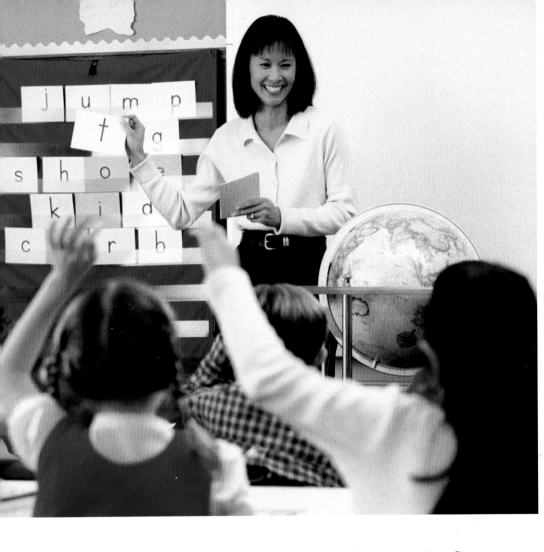

What does a teacher do?

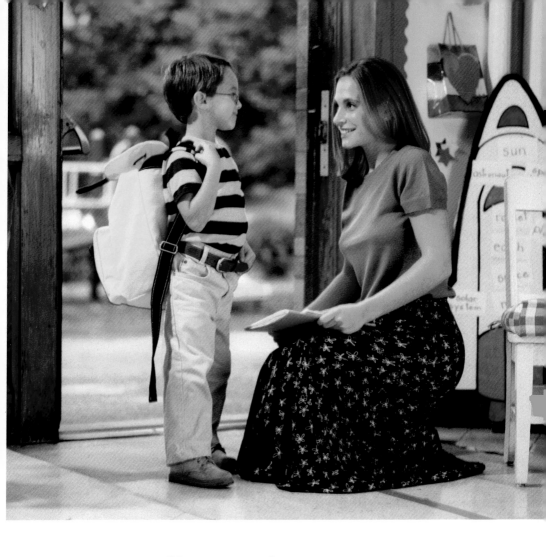

She welcomes.

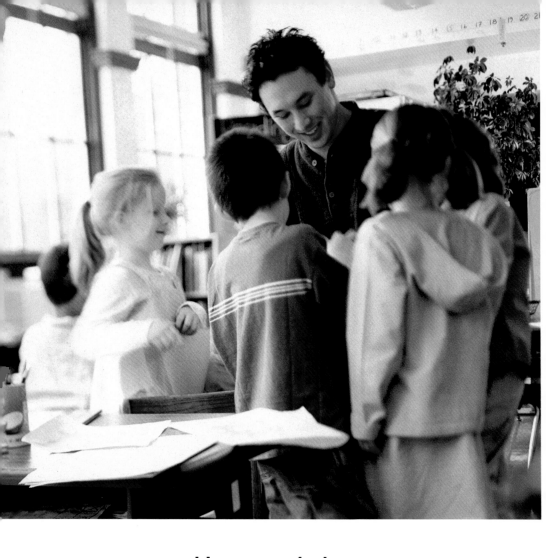

He explains.

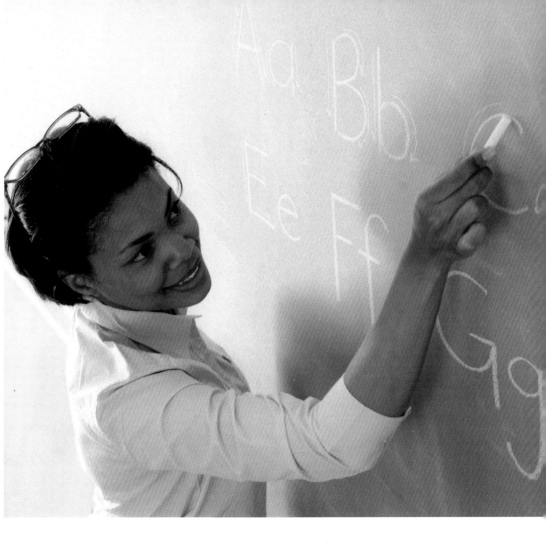

She writes.

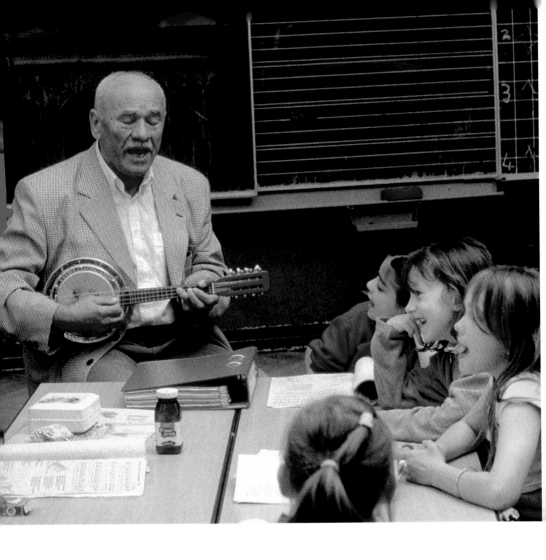

He sings.

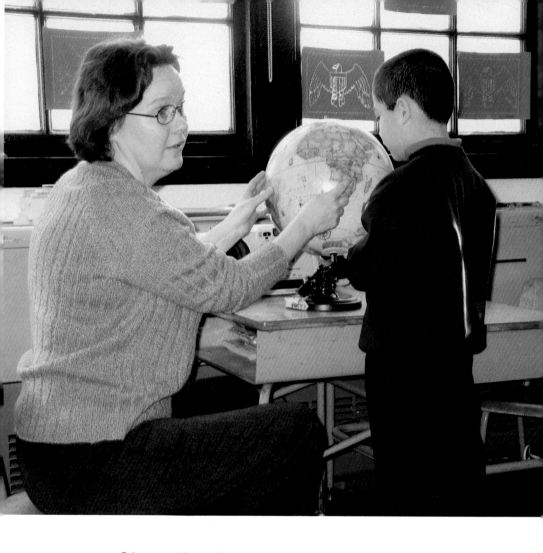

She helps me learn.

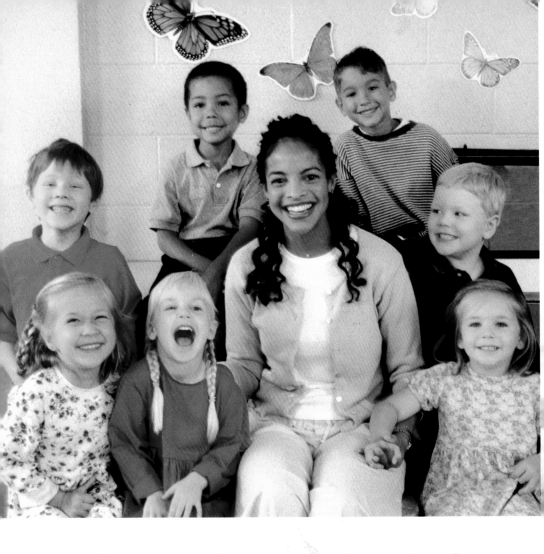

Do you know a teacher?